# STUDYING RUSSIAN

## ON

## COMPANY TIME

# STUDYING RUSSIAN ON COMPANY TIME

[POEMS IN CONTEXT]

CLEMENS STARCK

SILVERFISH REVIEW PRESS

. . .

The cover illustrations are reproduced from Soviet posters. The
front cover is a colored linocut by V. V. Lebedev, dating from
1920; the text reads "Work with your rifle beside you." On the
back cover is a detail from a 1919 lithograph by V. N. Deni, the
banner proclaiming "Long live worker-peasant Soviet power!"

Illustrations in the text are by Yu. Ushakov from a book on
northern Russian architecture: V. P. Orfinskii, *V mire skazochnoi
realnosti* (*In the World of Fairy-tale Reality*). Petrozavodsk: Izdatel'stvo
"Kareliya," 1972.

. . .

Some of these poems first appeared in: *ArtSpirit, Calapooya,
Jefferson Monthly, Как живут люди* (*Kak Zhivut Lyudi*), *Solo* and
*The Temple*.

"Friendship of the Peoples" and "The Museum of Russian History"
were recipients of a Carolyn Kizer Poetry Award in *Calapooya 19*.

Silverfish Review Press
P.O. Box 3541
Eugene, OR 97403

Умом Россию не понять,
Аршином общим не измерить;
У ней особенная стать—
В Россию можно только верить.

— Ф. И. Тютчев

You can't grasp Russia with your mind,
By ordinary means she can't be measured;
Her character is one-of-a-kind—
To fathom Russia you must believe.

— F. I. Tyutchev, 1866

# Contents

# [Prologue]

The day before I began studying Russian I had no intention whatsoever of studying Russian. It was the last thing on my mind. I had no particular interest in Russia or things Russian. Except for Chekhov, of course, and Dostoevsky. And learning the Cyrillic alphabet always seemed like it might be a good thing to do . . . But I was certainly not a Russophile.

It was September 1991. Astonishing events were taking place in eastern Europe. The coup attempt against Gorbachev had triggered what would have been unthinkable a few weeks earlier: the collapse of the Soviet Union. I was teaching an evening class at a local university and, as it turned out, I was to share an office with a visiting professor just off the plane from Moscow. Here was my chance to get a first-hand account of what was happening over there. Unfortunately, my office partner could speak very little English. Conversation was severely limited. So, in frustration, I offered to help her with her English, and as a joke I suggested that she could teach me Russian in return.

What began as a joke soon turned into an obsession, a daily practice. Phonetics. Grammar. Vocabulary. Something about the Russian language itself intrigued me. Trying to mouth the sounds of it was addictive. Only later, through the language, did I become fascinated with Russian culture and Russian history. And eventually I went to Russia.

The following pages are a little travelogue of sorts—some poems composed along the path of that continuing obsession, together with their context.

## [ "Studying Russian on Company Time" ]

As well as an obsession, studying Russian was for me a kind of subterfuge, a clandestine adventure. It was an unlikely thing to be doing, sitting in my truck at work, during coffee breaks and at lunch-time, flipping through Russian flash cards or conjugating Russian verbs aloud. It was a way of sneaking something completely arbitrary and improbable into my life. It felt almost illicit.

This first poem is conspiratorial in tone. It marks the 75th anniversary of the Bolshevik Revolution, an event that few were celebrating at the time.

By way of notes:

§ The period of Stalin's purges in the late '30s is known as the Great Terror. One of its victims was the Civil War hero and marshal of the Red Army, M. N. Tukhachevsky. The question may arise: Had the officer corps of the Red Army not been decimated by the purges, would the German tanks ever have gotten as far as Stalingrad in 1940?

§ In April 1917, shortly after the February Revolution had overthrown the tsar, V. I. Lenin returned from exile in Switzerland, arriving in St. Petersburg to a tumultuous welcome. The Finland Station is the *gare du nord* in St. Petersburg, the terminal for trains to and from the north.

§ The four Russian words in the poem are simply the first four days of the week: Monday, Tuesday, Wednesday, Thursday . . .

## Studying Russian on Company Time

Act like you're reading the sports page.
Pretend your textbook's a sandwich, and start eating it.
When the foreman asks what you're doing, ask him
if he knows where Olga and Ivan are.
Enunciate carefully: Olga
and Ivan are not in the library, Olga and Ivan
were not in the library,
Olga and Ivan
will not be in the library.

Now it is time for the Great Terror.
Take Tukhachevsky . . .
Take him and execute him.
Let the German tanks encircle Stalingrad. This
is an example of the perfective aspect
of the Russian verb.

When Vladimir Ilyich stepped off the train
at the Finland Station
a band struck up! Thousands cheered! Red and gold
        banners
flapped in the wind! It was a scene
out of a dream
dreamt by the Petersburg
League for the Liberation of the Working Class.

Seventy-five years!
Week follows week, day after day:
*ponedél'nik, ftórnik, sredá, chetvérg* . . . These are words
that bounce off the teeth. Remember,
the genitive singular of feminine nouns
is often the same
as the nominative plural.

Don't ask stupid questions.
Throw a quick glance over one shoulder, throw salt
over the other. Soon
you shall speak perfect Russian—
so flawlessly,
so fluently,
not even your comrades
will understand.

*7 November 1992*

[ "Making Do" ]

During the first few years I was lucky to have as tutors a succession of native Russian speakers. Mostly they were undergraduates at the university where I was working as a carpenter. One of them was a brilliant young biochemistry student from Leningrad (St. Petersburg). He was a demanding teacher, a real taskmaster who seemed to delight in red-penciling my written exercises. On the eve of his departure for graduate school in Washington, he invited me over for a farewell dinner.

He was living for a few weeks, rent-free, in a vacated apartment. It was completely bare. With makeshift furniture and rudimentary utensils we enjoyed a carefully prepared meal. I had brought a bottle of wine, and after dinner we sat on the floor, talking. About Russia. His English was excellent.

The siege of Leningrad and the massive suffering of an entire population, the ominous quality of life under Communist rule, the experience of terror, the present complete breakdown of the economic system—all this was a far remove from the idyllic ambiance of a summer evening in a small college-town in Oregon.

At one point he asked me about my poetry: How did a poem start? I've forgotten what I replied, but driving home late that night I started composing this next poem.

## MAKING DO

Two concrete blocks and a cardboard box
will serve as chairs and table.
A bare apartment needn't inconvenience you.
By all means
invite a friend. Drink wine. Converse. Discuss
the latest news
from Petersburg or Moscow.

If death is near, ask him to come—
he won't require
an extra chair. If there's no wine, water will do,
but keep the guest list small:
Vilyam Shekspir, Samu-el Beket . . . and don't forget
Chekhov, of course, master
of the banal.

After the guests arrive
make sure the door is barricaded, the windows
boarded up.
This is no picnic, citizens.
Deliberately, one by one,
light the three remaining candles.
Call them by their proper names:
Faith, Hope, Charity (or is it
Clarity?)

If there are no candles, darkness will do.
Hold hands, sing songs, tell dirty jokes,
or else exchange
scientific information.

But . . . if words fail, silence will do. Silence
will have to do, comrades,
silence and darkness . . .
It will not
be as bad as you think. It will be worse
than you can imagine.

*for Dmitri K.*

# ["Lenin's Typewriter"]

In the summer of 1994 I went to St. Petersburg. For three months I boarded with a Russian family, in their large apartment on Mayakovsky Street, just four doors off Nevsky Prospekt. I studied Russian. I explored the city. By 1994 most of the trappings of Soviet Communism had already disappeared, like so much window dressing. But traces of Lenin were still everywhere in evidence: busts and monuments, bronze and marble plaques embedded in the sides of buildings . . .

The Smolny Institute had been a women's boarding school in tsarist times. It was taken over by the Bolsheviks in 1917 and served as their headquarters. Momentous decisions were made here in the weeks and months following the Revolution. Lenin had his office here. Later the building was preserved as a museum, one of the hallowed places of Soviet power.

Our tour guide pointed proudly to Lenin's typewriter on a stand next to his desk. It was an Underwood! The American company must have had a franchise to produce Russian-language typewriters in pre-revolutionary Russia. I thought to myself: How strange, that the Russian Revolution should have been orchestrated on an American-brand typewriter!

## LENIN'S TYPEWRITER

Sparrows and pigeons. No squirrels. Crows. A tank
on a pedestal. T-34.
Photograph this,
with the weeds overtaking the wrought-iron fence
and the shattered statue
of a Young Pioneer.
Remember,
first there was the Revolution,
then there was the War.

Defenders of Leningrad, take your positions.
One with a shovel, another a rifle—
you shall be cast in bronze.

Trash on the sidewalk along the canal.
Dogshit and broken glass.
A marble plaque commemorates
V. I. Lenin's having hidden out here once,
July of 1917.
             And in the Smolny
is Lenin's typewriter—
squatting there like some infernal dream machine,
still spitting out in Russian letters
recipes for revolution.

Clackety-clackety-clack . . .

Inkstand, green felt, a gooseneck lamp
and the trusty Underwood—
what more do you need to change the world?

But those prescriptions went awry.
They're selling them on the street for souvenirs.
Come to Russia, and bring cash! Maybe
you can make a deal—
on an icon or a cathedral,
a typewriter
or a tank.

*St. Petersburg*
*August 1994*

# ["The Museum of Russian History"]

Trying to grasp another language is tantalizing. It requires considerable guesswork, becoming itself an act of imagination. The museum described in the next poem is a fiction, a metaphor, a composite of the various museums I visited in Russia. The tour is a fantasy. In fact, Russian history itself is a kind of strange fairy tale or fantasy. As witness the lives of the three poets mentioned:

§ Aleksandr Blok (1880–1921), greatest of the Russian Symbolists, is to modern Russian poetry what Rilke is to German, or Yeats to English poetry. He died soon after the Revolution, disheartened by the turn it had taken.

§ Nikolai Gumilyov (1886–1921), traveller, adventurer, husband of Anna Akhmatova, founder of the Acmeist movement—this "Last Knight of Russia" was not allowed to attend Blok's funeral and was executed by the Bolsheviks shortly thereafter.

§ Sergei Yesenin (1895–1925), a peasant's son from the Russian countryside, had a meteoric rise to fame in the years immediately preceding the Revolution. Later he was married to the American dancer Isadora Duncan, and still later hanged himself in a Leningrad hotel room after writing a last poem with his own blood.

# THE MUSEUM OF RUSSIAN HISTORY

Our tour guide speaks in rapid Russian
that I pretend to understand.
"This first exhibit," she explains,
"is a tableau
of one of our most famous Russian customs."
Blindfolded, against the wall,
comrade Stalin with his pipe
is smiling
at the firing squad.

"That's interesting!" we observe,
and go on to the next:
an enormous panorama entitled *The Defense
of Sevastopol.* In the foreground
Galina Stepanovna
(my landlady) is crouched beside a campfire,
besieged by wounded soldiers.
She's busy preparing
cabbage soup.

Then suddenly—heroic music,
sound effects . . . the thin metallic voices
of the poets, Gumilyov and Blok,
barely audible
above the crash and din of Revolution.
Yesenin is there too,
a life-size wax replica in peasant costume,
passionately reciting verses
to a birch tree.

The axe, the whip, an icon;
gilded cherubs and the twisted wreckage
of the German tanks . . .
It's complicated, and the language
is hard to follow.
In any case, the tour is brief.
"There's more, of course," our guide assures us,
"but it
is not for foreigners."

["Friendship of the Peoples"]

One thing leads to another, and in January 1996 I returned to the former Soviet Union, this time to its southern extremity, the Crimea. I was in charge of a group of American students taking classes at Simferopol State University. I took classes too.

The woman with whom I boarded for four months worked as a director at the local television station. One day she invited me to go along on the expedition described in the following poem. The purpose of the trip was to document on film the last days of a collective farm. The farm, with its idealized Soviet-style name, was soon to be "privatized." The dreams of socialism were coming to an end.

## FRIENDSHIP OF THE PEOPLES

Six empty vodka bottles on the table,
and the remnants of a feast. On the collective farm
called *Druzhba Narodov*—Friendship
of the Peoples—
it's a holiday. The director
is Ukranian.
His name is Peter.

There's singing, of course, and speeches;
and for the young folk
a judo tournament. The local
militia is there,
and sportsmen from the school. There's also the man
who can raise a chair above his head
with his teeth.
                    What teeth! What a neck!
— "A real animal!" says Galina
disparagingly.

Galina works for Crimean Television. We are filming
an episode in the series *How People Live*
on a collective farm.
"It's altogether different in America," I say (in Russian,
trying hard to sound casual). "There's not
such merriment,
and the vodka's not so good."

Later we tour the rice fields
in a brand-new Russian jeep. Tractors
are dragging enormous plumes of dust across the steppe,
obscuring the horizon.

Now the cameraman is shooting *us*—Peter and me—
standing on the dike, absorbed in conversation. Peter
is explaining everything.
I'm listening
intently. I can hardly
understand a word.

[ "Druzhba Narodov" ]

Many months after returning from the Crimea I received a letter in Russian from my landlady asking that I send her "the poem about our visit to the collective farm." She said that the footage of the director and me on the dike engaged in conversation was excellent. They were going to use it in the film, and also wanted to include my poem.

How did she know about the poem? I had just finished working on it the week before! It was uncanny. I must have mentioned jokingly once that someday maybe I would write such a poem ... But in any case, the poem was in English—how was she going to read it? So, as an exercise, I decided to translate it. Here it is in Russian, corrected and polished with the help of my various Russian teachers. I've never seen the film.

## Дружба народов

На столе
шесть пустых бутылок из-под водки,
и остатки банкета. Сегодня праздник
в колхозе,
который называется «Дружба народов» (Friendship
of the Peoples). Директор —
украинец.
Имя — Петр.

Здесь пение есть, конечно, и речи.
А для молодежи
турнир дзюдо. Местная
милиция присутствует,
и спортсмены из школы. Есть и мужчина,
который может зубами поднять стул
над головой.
        Какие зубы! Какая шея!
—Настоящий зверь!—говорит Галина
неодобрительно.

Галина работает на крымском телевидении.
Мы снимаем
эпизод из серии «Как живут люди»
в колхозе.
—В Америке совсем по-другому,—говорю я (по-русски,
пытаясь звучать непринужденно). —Там
не так весело,
и водка не такая хорошая.

Позже мы объезжаем рисовые поля
на новеньком русском джипе. Трактора
тащат огромные перья пыли через степь,
затемняя горизонт.

Сейчас операмор н а с снимает — Петра и меня —
пока мы стоим на дамбе и разговарываем. Петр
объясняет все.
Я слушаю
напряженно. Я почти не понял
ни слова.

— Клеменс Старк
(перевод автора с
английского языка)

["Protokol"]

The Russian word *protokol* has come to have a different sense than the corresponding English "protocol." The English word usually refers to rules prescribing etiquette and correct procedure, whereas in Russian a *protokol* (pronounced pra-ta-KOHL) is a record of proceedings, as evidence to be submitted in a court of law. Or simply, the minutes of a meeting. Russian also makes a verb of it: *protokolirovat'*, "to protocolize", to compile a *protokol*. Which is what the police official is doing in this next poem.

In part, the poem is a tribute to Mikhail Zoshchenko (1895–1958), the classic writer of Soviet satire. His sketches and short stories published in the '20s are comic masterpieces. His name is pronounced ZOSH-shenk-uh.

Riding the bus in a Russian city is not something easily described. The number of persons squeezed into a Russian bus at times exceeds the limits of physical probability. It is a truly collective experience.

# PROTOKOL

### 1.

I'm sitting in the police station, telling
my story.
Tat'yana is there too, helping.
Six times I tell the story, each time
to a different person,
and each time (if I may say so) the story
gets better.

I was on a trolleybus. The trolleybus was crowded.
Very crowded.
I was conscious of my body,
and of the five other bodies pressing
against mine.

I had just bought a book. Several books.
One was by Zoshchenko.
He's one of my favorite authors.

2.

Now a man is writing down my story.
With a fountain pen.
At a desk that looks like it was manufactured
before the Revolution.
Or maybe just after the Revolution, at about the time
Zoshchenko
was telling his stories.

Another man is at another desk,
a cigarette in one hand.
The index finger of the other is jabbing
at a typewriter.
He's typing
someone else's story.

Tomorrow is a holiday—
Victory Day. I was on my way
to the university.
I had to wait a long time for a trolleybus.
That's why it was so crowded.

3.

The man whose job it is
to write down my story
ponders before he writes. Each sentence
is premeditated.
His composure is almost beatific. His penmanship
is also quite remarkable.

The other man
is having trouble with his typewriter.
The carriage has jammed. *"Mashínka slomálas'!"*—
Typewriter's broke!
He pounds the desk.
He pounds the typewriter.

The room is drab and bare.
Green wallpaper. A floral pattern. Water-stained.
It looks like it too
dates from the time of Zoshchenko.

4.

Finally it's my turn to write. I write
what I am told,
and I write very carefully also, because
I am writing in Russian.

Tat'yana gives me some leaves to chew.
They taste like chicory.
*"Óchen' polézni!"* she says—Very healthy!—and goes on
to inform me that what I have just written
is to affirm
that what the man has written
is correct.

And it is correct. It is my story.

5.

Now the man is copying what he has written
onto a second sheet of paper.
He has that look
of a missionary, zealously translating
Paul's Epistles
into some outlandish tongue.

Otherwise, he seems like a reasonable man.
He smiles sometimes
and asks me questions.
The same questions he asked before.

I try to tell my story
as simply as I can.
I was on a trolleybus. The Number Four
trolleybus. I got on
at Lenin Square.

6.

As it turns out,
there is a third sheet of paper to be inscribed
with my story. But this time
my story is abridged.
Only the important parts are told.

There's little likelihood
my wallet will be returned, the man concedes,
but still,
we have to do what we are doing—
it's protocol.

And he takes from his briefcase
another sheet of paper.
This one is not plain, however, like the others.
This one is a form to be filled out,
and at the top
is written, in Russian letters:

PROTOKOL

7.

After three hours and forty minutes
we say good-bye.
I thank the man. I thank Tat'yana for her help.
And I set out, on foot,
across the boundless distances of Russia.

A metaphor, of course. In fact,
I'm walking along Kievskaya, trying *not* to look
like a foreigner.

Suddenly, for no reason,
I recall the story of the Peach Blossom Spring.
It's not Russian, it's an old
Chinese story.
But it's a good story.
Zoshchenko would have liked it.

## ["Foxtrot U-521"]

As a boy in upstate New York in the early '50s I belonged to the Ground Observer Corps. It was a branch of Civil Defense. From a rotunda atop the tallest building in Rochester, we watched for enemy planes. We all knew that if they came they would be coming from the north, sweeping down from the Arctic across Canada. They would be Russian.

At that time many people were building bomb shelters in their backyards. In school the siren would sound for an air-raid drill . . .

Now it was 1997. The Cold War was over. History plays some strange tricks.

§ Emily Carr (1875–1941) is one of Canada's best known and best loved artists. Her intense and compelling nature paintings have been compared to those of Georgia O'Keeffe, Edvard Munch and Vincent van Gogh.

# FOXTROT U-521

When I was in Vancouver
I never did
see the Russian submarine,
although it was on display, open to the public
from 9:30 to 6:30 every day of the week
except Monday.

Instead
I visited the Art Museum—
an exhibit of paintings by Emily Carr.

The paintings were memorable;
but even without having seen it, I can picture
the submarine, a sleek
steel cigar,
probing the waters of the Pacific
with its deadly arsenal, and its crew of seventy-five . . .
Foxtrot U-521.
On patrol.
Engaged in secret surveillance.

All those years! The fear of imminent catastrophe!
And now the sub is docked
at a quay in New Westminster, just another
overpriced
tourist attraction.

Clemens Starck, a 1998 Witter Bynner Fellow at Willamette University, received both the William Stafford Memorial Poetry Award and the Oregon Book Award in Poetry for his collection, *Journeyman's Wages* (Story Line Press, 1995). For thirty-five years, Starck has earned his living as a journeyman carpenter. He lives in rural Oregon.

This book was designed by Joseph Bednarik using New Baskerville and Times Cyrillic typefaces. The major portion of the design work was accomplished under exceptionally clear skies in Port Townsend, Washington, on the 81st anniversary of the Bolshevik Revolution.